RICH

MOTHERF$CKER

HOW TO BECOME A BAD BOY WHO FINISHES RICH BY CREATING REBELLIOUS WEALTH BECAUSE YOU ARE A BAD ASS CEO

Ray Bolden

RICH MOTHERF$CKER
Copyright © 2017 Ray Bolden. All rights reserved.

The book you are about to read is based on the experience of its author, Ray Bolden as well as information he has read or come in contact with. Mr. Bolden does not hold any legal, accounting, or college degrees nor does he or has he ever held a securities license.

Disclaimer
This publication is designed to provide accurate and authoritative information in regard to the subject matter covered. It is sold with the understanding that neither the author nor the publisher is engaged in rendering legal, investment, accounting or other professional advice. Any actions with regard to the information contained in this book should be undertaken only with the advice and counsel of a trained legal professional. If legal advice or other expert assistance is required, the services of a competent professional person should be sought.

The entire project is underwritten by the author. His views and interpretations of the findings may not necessarily be the same as those of the organizations that market the brands that are mentioned in this work.

ISBN-13: 978-0692077429 (Bold Ambition Worldwide, LLC)
ISBN-10: 0692077421

Dedication

This is dedicated to my younger less financially educated self. The guy who foreclosed on his first house…the guy who ate Beanie Weenies for dinner because he only had $150 left at the end of the month and couldn't make ends meet…The guy who sat on the back of his car with his yellow legal pad figuring out how to budget and pay off debt…The guy who sat on the edge of his bed with his head in his hands drained and frustrated continually saying to himself, "there's got to be a better way"…We did it!!

Author's Note

I was mentally and financially trapped and I wasn't in control of my life, so I became obsessed with learning ways to create true freedom. Out of necessity, I discovered that I was a *RICH MOTHERF$CKER*. Your mission should you choose to accept it is to discover who you really are.

Table of Contents

Preface

Complete the following sentence: "To me, *RICH MOTHERF$CKER* means..." I know it's a complex question, and, not surprisingly, people have varying opinions on it. What's your definition? Some of you might be thinking that this is focusing on the negative. It's not! Although you might not self-identify, I actually take it as a compliment. To me the term *RICH MOTHERF$CKER* is simply another avenue of authenticity. Why? Because we all have picture perfect dreams of how our lives will turn out, but life doesn't quite work like that. To some degree we are all sleepwalking through our lives. Many of us lead a programmed life. Much of what we do is determined by our culture, family, values, friends, education, career path and financial status, but freedom is a conundrum and a treasure. It's neither neat nor logical so I decided that I wouldn't live my life in the hope that someday I would magically dream my way into financial freedom. I refused to. Contrary to what you are thinking right now, this is not a philosophical discussion. Economic empowerment is one of the most rebellious and incendiary acts that an individual can perform. If you are playing by the rules, you have already lost. In an effort to free myself and play my own game within the game, I came up with disruptive ideas that lead to extremely wonderful experiences. I walked many paths and lived a very colorful life. I got a lot of it wrong, but I also got a lot of it right. So, I write this book to begin a conversation not to lay down the law.

Every now and then, some people get it in their heads that they deserve the right to walk free in the world. They start believing that they are worthy of the best of the best. That's why you picked up this book. *RICH MOTHERF$CKER* speaks to everyone who wants to control their destiny and get out of survival mode. It's for those of you who feel that there is creativity and greatness in you, but you just need a little help getting started. It's about enlightenment and it's a state of mind that helps you see the truth. Not some far off day of hope, but the here and now! It's about fighting for the freedom to define yourself on your terms and it's about letting go of the old ideas that helped you survive and embracing new ones to help you and everyone around you thrive. Life is not meant to be a long series of unfelt and undirected experiences. We are not meant to be zombies, slaves or unconscious animals trapped in the dumbness of a system of oppression that has given us an identity of subordination as a way to see ourselves. Doesn't it strike you as odd that you can go through 12-20 years of education in this country and never learn how money really works, who makes the rules or how to play the game? It's time to become more alert and engaged in the world of money. With that said, the question now becomes: "What would becoming a *RICH MOTHERF$CKER* and obtaining financial freedom do for you?" People are asking for someone, anyone to come save their lives. My objective is to teach what I have learned on my journey. It's a process of self-creation in a society that has already defined you and it's resisting that definition because it denies you.

One of the most rewarding things I feel blessed to do with my financial freedom is to help others obtain their financial freedom so that they don't have to make choices based on money or obligation. There are plenty of books merely about sacrificing, saving and deferring your life to the future, but *RICH MOTHERF$CKER* is not merely about defense, it's about offense as well. This book gives you an opportunity to increase your means. You will learn that it is about you, your attitude about yourself and your values, not just about being rich. So, remove your rose-colored glasses and think objectively. Change is hard and building a life of true economic empowerment and self-reliance will require you to become new, but it's not beyond you to do so. We strive to create the best version of ourselves because there exists an indistinct possibility that through will and creativity we can alter reality. But sometimes we need something, or someone to help us believe that the effort is worthwhile. So, I've written furious, sobering words to help you channel the *RICH MOTHERF$CKER* spirit to achieve great things regardless of your background. What I can tell you is this: Everyone has the opportunity to become a *RICH MOTHERF$CKER*, but not everyone is taking that opportunity. So, I'm going to show you how to think like an entrepreneur and an owner and I'm going to help you find the seed of self-reliance in yourself and nurture it… whatever it may be so that you can know the kind of peace and security that financial independence brings. If you wake up worried about money, this book will be of huge significance for you because this book is not based on theory, good ideas or a new philosophy. It is the result of years of experience living the principles presented here so please understand that this book didn't just happen, it evolved. It gives you questions to ask yourself and gives you ways to apply this to your life and discover what you can do. This approach has never let me down and it has made a tremendous difference in my life. Hell, the appendix sections are worth the investment in this book alone. You have a wonderful opportunity; will you take yours? The fight won't be easy, but it will be worth it. Continually read this book and embrace the power of the *RICH MOTHERF$CKER* mindset presented here and the odds are in your favor.

RICH MOTHERF$CKER

Function:

Noun

1. Peace of mind. Fiscal bliss.

2. A clear, relaxed relationship with money.

3. Empowered, self-reliant, self-actualized and free.

4. Being free from the fog, fear and fanaticism so many feel about money.

5. Anyone who applies financial literacy and financial independence thinking to his or her life.

6. Having an income sufficient for your basic needs and comforts from a source other than paid employment.

RICH MOTHERF$CKER!

"I didn't invent the game, I'm just playing it in my own way!!"

~ Ray Bolden

Introduction

THE FREEST BLACK MAN IN THE WORLD

How many of you are free? The fact that you have to think about it is all the answer you need. Mediocrity is not an option for me, I don't want that, and neither should you. You are going to win. Can you feel it? Can you see it? If not, go back and read that sentence again. As I sit here writing this introduction, my heart and spirit are racing at the speed of light to get this message to anyone who is sick and tired of not being free. I started writing this book when I was angry, long before I had written *BAD BOYS FINI$H RICH, REBELLIOU$ WEALTH* or *BAD A$$ CEO*, because I had hit that point in my life where I was asking who do I need to become and what do I need to do to be financially free. I wanted to have the opportunity myself to determine what I wanted. That meant economic opportunity. I wanted access to the full complement of privileges and benefits. My rage could be harnessed as a weapon for revolution. There was only one direction that my ambition pointed. It meant something special to me even before I could articulate what that something was because I hated the idea of being defined by society's definition of who I was supposed to be. I loved the idea of feeling that powerful, so I looked deeply into my life and what was driving me most...I just wanted freedom. Did you know that It's harder for a child born in America to move out of poverty than it is for children in most other developed countries? I wanted to take full advantage of the opportunities I had, and I just wanted to be able to do what I wanted, without financial worry. Ultimately, it's really freedom we're all after. The money, the status and the security because we're counting on it taking us to a place where we can feel a sense of freedom that makes sense to us. I wish I could say I was making some grand rebellious statement, but without the ability to be whole and financially secure on your own terms, there can be no freedom and no liberation. So, it's ok to think outside of the box. Especially the box that has imprisoned you. The simple question is: "What are you willing to do to live a life that meets your definition of true freedom?"

RICH MOTHERF$CKER is about human potential and about not being defined by what you do, but rather by who you choose to become because you always, always, always, have a choice that you create for yourself. It's about unveiling who you are and who you are capable of becoming. In this book, I want to teach you everything that I wish I had known when I was younger, but it's not one size fits all. It will be different for each of you. For some it will come easy and for some it will take extra focus and effort. My personal goal for all of you is that if you understand who you are, you will know how to deal when it comes to generating an income because you will have a self-worth that's entirely different than what's been perpetuated by society. I want you to recognize that right here, right now, as you read this book, you are in the process of changing your view of what's possible and achieving your dreams. The land of opportunity doesn't have to be the land of missed opportunities. We have a choice. We've always had those choices, but instead of seizing the moment and moving forward, we have been diverted by the fear that has kept us spiraling in recurring themes of disfranchisement and financial illiteracy. It's time to defuse the power of subordination and it's time to move into the future. So the moral of this story is to make sure you are not too conditioned to stay trapped because the less freedom you feel you have in your life and in your choices, the more trapped you feel. Wealth is often thought of as an unattainable number that doesn't apply to most of us, but that's a notion that needs to be retired. So, it's not about whether you are going to become a *RICH MOTHERF$CKER*; it's about when you are going to become a *RICH MOTHERF$CKER*. You can have the money, the security, the comfort, the luxury, the big toys and the fancy vacations. More importantly, you can have the freedom to be you, to be happy, to be fulfilled and to do whatever you want. Nothing mentioned here is too far beyond your imagination. What matters is that you look deep inside and find out what gives you the ultimate freedom in your life. *RICH MOTHERF$CKER* symbolizes freedom. It is a lifestyle upgrade and expansion. Each person who follows this program will gain something unique that adds to his or her life. You will reconnect with old dreams and find ways to realize them. Money will cease to be an issue. You will have the intellectual an emotional space to take on issues of greater importance and you will be inwardly confident and outwardly self-aware. Millions of people are victims of the economy rather than participants, so I realize there will be those who read this book and see no relationship between self-sufficiency, financial literacy and economic empowerment, but make no mistake, this is a book about winning.

It's rare to have people look at your body of work, think clearly and have a full premise and understanding without contradicting or looking for holes in your philosophy or teachings. I have struggled and gone through the same things as many others. I took risks and I leaped before looking a few times. I've even failed miserably and started over many times along the way. But I researched endlessly, and I found a problem that I and others experienced that I was uniquely qualified to solve. I have been through writer's block and I have also been through many, many times where I wasn't sure of myself. Now I'm at the point where I live very comfortably off the income generated by solving my problems and that gave me freedom. I am embarrassed that I have kept this book from you due to delays on my part because I procrastinated, but this truth-telling book will push your boundaries on things and move you into different types of frontiers that hadn't been tested before. At the end of each chapter, I'll be laying out some assignments. These are crucial to your financial future. My hope is to offer a vision to promote economic freedom and help as many people as I can achieve their financial targets and have freedom and choices in their lives. There is this thing called the American Dream but keep in mind that it only seems to apply to very few people. Are you prepared to go against what you thought was the traditional way of doing things? Why? Because there's also this mindset called *RICH MOTHERF$CKER* that can produce financial freedom. But you don't get it by sitting around waiting for it and it doesn't come to you by chance. It's a matter of choice. It's something you got to go out and get.

PART ONE

Be whoever you want to be. There are no rules

RICH MOTHERF$CKER!

"Let me be perfectly clear, I don't give a fuck at this point. My life don't work like that. I can make anything happen!"

~ Diddy

Chapter One

THE RICHEST MOTHERF$CKER THAT YOU WILL EVER MEET IS IN THE MIRROR

(Stop watching other people's lives and start living your own)

The greatest misconception about creating wealth and success is that there are certain career paths that you have to take to be successful. This is where people fail. They continually move from this perceived opportunity to that perceived opportunity hoping, wishing and begging for success then when it doesn't happen they blame what it was that they attempted to do rather than taking a deep-rooted, hard look at themselves. When defining success, we should go beyond the normal parameters and look at what real success is to us individually. If I asked a million people, I would get a million different answers. Every one of us would have our unique version of what we would like to achieve in our lives. The cardinal rule of success, whether that be to obtain wealth or otherwise is that "It's not what you have to do, but who you chose to become", that will lead you towards the life that you desire. In other words, it's about self-discovery and molding yourself into the person that you want to be through financial literacy and success education. In short you are the product of your mind. Every thought and belief you have stored inside, or that transitions, even fleetingly, through your mind shapes your experience of life. Your values and beliefs shape your perception of reality and as a result your ability to achieve anything in life. So, if you are wishing to achieve financial freedom which is only a small part of what it takes to being truly free in life, then having the right mindset is vital.

RICH MOTHERF$CKER is the term I use to describe myself and others who push the boundaries of other people's rules because we know the life that we want to live and look deep inside ourselves to find out what gives us the ultimate freedom to be who we want to be and do what we want to do. It's a mindset and the sum of the way that you think about the positive things that you want to achieve or acquire. It is how your values and beliefs shape your thoughts. It's whatever makes you happy, successful and prosperous and its whatever fixed idea you have in your mind. It can be whatever you want it to be. It's is not about becoming something that you aren't, it's about unveiling who you have been the entire time.

The world is full of well educated, highly trained and extraordinary people like yourself who have yet to experience the life that they desire. It's not that you aren't smart, you are. What you lack more than anything is that you have yet to define yourself as a *RICH MOTHERF$CKER*. Yeah, I know you probably really, really, really don't like this term, but your chances for wealth, success and self-discovery are greater the more you are out of step with society. People are unconscious of the presence and power of the *RICH MOTHERF$CKER* mindset inside themselves. This is a mental depiction of growth and development-both personal and professional and it's a testament to the fact that anyone can reshape their thinking, can reshape their life and continue to live that reshaped life. This helps to reinforce positive ideas into your subconscious mind and causes you to clearly define yourself in positive terms. Once you have this knowledge of yourself, you are rich in every way because you can take that knowledge and be what you want to be, do what you want to do and have what you want to have. This is an extremely valuable tool to have in your toolbox. One that allows you to recognize and evaluate opportunities in a global context and better understand the people you encounter in business, academia and other settings. With this tool, ultimately you will be able to deal with any person on any level in any category and get much more of what you want out of life. It's not so much a matter of being exceptional compared to others; it's a matter of how effectively and efficiently you define yourself and utilize what you have. This means putting your talents, skills and available resources to the best possible use. Keep in mind that freedom, power, wealth and success can be defined in many ways. We are the tool that creates our life including our finances. All things considered, when you are ready to be free... financially or otherwise you have a choice and if you forget you have that choice then you might as well be in a cage, because you are not using the freedom of the *RICH MOTHERF$CKER* presence within you at all.

THE SUBTLE ART OF
BEING A RICH MOTHERF$CKER

✓ RICH MOTHERF$CKERs increase their income by reducing their expenses!

✓ RICH MOTHERF$CKERs learn to be profitable no matter what the economy does!

✓ RICH MOTHERF$CKERs imagine and create with a sense of power and inevitability!

✓ RICH MOTHERF$CKERs understand that it is their choice alone to move toward freedom!

✓ RICH MOTHERF$CKERs secure their advantage and increase their power!

✓ RICH MOTHERF$CKER's financial education revolves around their values and their lifestyles!

✓ RICH MOTHERF$CKERs increase their savings and are able to live happily within their means!

✓ RICH MOTHERF$CKERs have the intellectual and emotional space to take on issues of greater importance!

✓ RICH MOTHERF$CKERs choose who they are above and beyond their immediate impulses, needs and social pressures!

✓ RICH MOTHERF$CKERs learn how to distinguish between the essentials and the excess in all areas of their lives and how to unburden themselves!

✓ RICH MOTHERF$CKERs seize unique opportunities to structure a system to their sole advantage!

✓ RICH MOTHERF$CKERs understand how money works. They know the rules of the game and they play to win!

✓ RICH MOTHERF$CKERs understand the importance of learning; they are always feeding their mind!

✓ RICH MOTHERF$CKERs master the ability to focus relentlessly on their ambitions and act decisively toward them!

✓ RICH MOTHERF$CKERs genuinely express the type of person they want to be, live the life they truly want to live and leave the legacy that they desire!

RICH MOTHERF$CKER is an intangible. It's security, happiness and peace of mind. At its essence it is a measuring device... that measure or your mindset. It's an action word and it begins with a thought, an idea and a belief. It's a function of letting go of any self-doubt and allowing ourselves to be unique, powerful and authentic. It's about not believing society's opinion of who you are supposed to be. I choose to remain true to who I am and where my dreams direct me because the *RICH MOTHEF$CKER* mindset changed my life. To be more precise, specifically it ignited my financial education and expanded my concept of money. Having a *RICH MOTHERF$CKER* mindset means having self-respect. If you value and esteem yourself correctly, all the world will respond to you as a winner.

TOMORROW IS NOT JUST GOING TO BE ANOTHER DAY, ANOTHER DOLLAR

The attempt to declare your presence to the world is the common theme beneath nearly every boast and every metaphor so to obtain the type of financial independence you've been dreaming about all your life, you must learn to develop a *"RICH MOTHERF$CKER* mindset." I'm in the business of positively conditioning people's minds for success and I make no apology for saying that if you believe in this mindset, you can be what you want to be, have what you want to have and do what you want to do. If you open your mind to this idea of success, you will be motivated, and you will be lead to do those things that will make you successful. Being a *RICH MOTHERF$CKER* means you experience life according to your belief in yourself. We are all just people trying to life a good life, but some of us believe that we can do anything. So, when I am asked why I call myself a *RICH MOTHERF$CKER*, my answer is, "Because I knew the type of guy I wanted to be." What about you? Now I must admit that when I first started I had no idea how to play the game of money, but I knew I couldn't simply just sit around and hope and pray for someone to show me how. So, I took the opportunity to publicly anoint myself with a new identity...an alter ego for my creative endeavors. I decided not to wait for somebody else to do me the honor because doubts, fears and other people's rules are no match for a *RICH MOTHERF$CKER*. It required a certain audacity, but we all have seeds of greatness inside us, yet only some of us will allow ourselves to grow. I became wealth conscious without any help or support. I simply knew that I had been conditioned to be an employee and that my current financial situation was a by-product of this conditioning. I began to think critically about my upbringing and the larger social and educational system and began to challenge my own existence. It forced me to rethink everything I once believed. I really had no other choice because I was serious about my personal growth. It all began with a very simple question: "Who do I want to become?" My answer, a *RICH MOTHERF$CKER*! It was nothing short of liberating for me because whatever we make ourselves believe, we can experience. It depends on how you program your mind and how you program your consciousness. What I'm teaching you is simple, but you'd be surprised how few people use it. The mass of people are too mentally lazy to think for themselves. They listen to the radio, watch TV and the news and are influenced by what the media tells them to think. They are unconsciously being programmed. What you experience in life depends on what ideas you accept and reject. In life, you only get what you want based on your knowledge of who you are, and who you subconsciously know you can become. Today, my books are a monument that say I was here and that I didn't waste the time that was given to me so *RICH MOTHERF$CKER* is for everyone who is willing to take the time and make the effort. It's for everyone who has a concept in his/her mind for a better life… an idea of a better way to live and an idea of having and enjoying more.

IT'S INCREDIBLE
AND IT'S HAPPENING

You may as I have, find things that you say and do taken out of context, misunderstood, misinterpreted, dismissed or just outright ignored. So please know that I regard this transition as a difficult one because the *RICH MOTHERF$CKER* mindset is not a traditional way of thinking and acting. The key to success lies in your ability to personalize the elements of the model and make them your own. Ultimately, my model must become your model. Otherwise, you stand little chance of achieving the kind of life that I have described. If you have adopted the traditional model of success but want to play your own game within the game, it's wise to create your own model. The way I see it, ordinary success is a real good job, but real success is the freedom to live a great lifestyle. To some people this may sound egotistical, but I'd like to quote Chad Johnson, AKA Ocho Cinco here, "You have to have some type of selfishness to you in anything that you do to be successful at it. Sometimes that selfishness is mistaken for arrogance or cockiness, but ain't nobody humble out here. Cause humble ain't getting you nowhere. You can't be humble and be great because you have to have a certain drive and tenacity about you to get the damn job done." This is knowing the basis of your power...your oneness with your mindset and your oneness with your *RICH MOTHERF$CKER* mindset is your basis for your power. If you believe in yourself the doors of opportunity will swing open for you, so you have to develop the proper mindset. An interesting thing happens once you accept the idea. Once you open your mind and accept the idea, an inflow of other correlating ideas begin to take place. Everything will begin to come to you, but you must accept the possibility first. Wealth awaits all those who discover their true identity. If I can get you to live with this feeling, with this realization, with this consciousness, with this awareness, you will be able to say to yourself, "I have something that nobody can take away from me!" You are in the biggest game of all...the game of money and I know you want to win. In order to win you have to believe in the best for yourself. You have a power within you that says fuck the obstructions that are in front of you, you can make anything happen and *RICH MOTHERF$CKER* can be a vehicle for you to create the lifestyle that you desire provided you take the time and effort to grasp what it can do for you.

"RICH MOTHERF$CKER" – EXERCISE APPENDIX - A

Everything is a condition of the mind. The idea comes first and then the manifestation of that idea. You can't be, you can't do and you can't have anything until you first have the idea of it in your mind. Whatever you believe about yourself seals your destiny and whatever you believe about yourself brings you success or failure. This is the pure self-psychology of your *RICH MOTHERF$CKER* mindset. By truthfully answering the following questions you can take your lifestyle and your personal finances to the next level. How you answer these questions will help you to identify what's missing in your financial life and help you to determine where you want to go, and what resources you need to leverage for help.

- How do you define yourself? (Take some time with this & explain in detail)

- What idea of who you are, are you planting in your mind?

- How important are self-awareness and self-discovery to you?

- How can your definition of yourself help you to take control of your life and your finances?

- What kind of mind-set do you wake up with each day? How can you improve it?

You are never going to experience anything better than, or anything other than your own definition. Whatever you want to be, define yourself as that because whatever you define yourself as, that is what you become.

PART TWO

Go left when everybody else goes right

RICH MOTHERF$CKER!

"Financial freedom my only hope. Fuck living rich and dying broke!"

~ Jay Z

Chapter Two

INVENT MONEY THAT ALREADY EXISTS

(A higher income doesn't
guarantee financial freedom)

In America we place more importance on how much a person makes than how much they keep. You've been hoodwinked to believe that wealth can be created by recklessly trusting in the uncontrollable and unpredictable. Though it's natural to stress about money, many people are suffering from full-fledged financial anxiety, and a big reason boils down to a general lack of money management. Getting rich is about more than making a lot of money... it's about managing the money that you have. No matter which guidelines you follow, most experts agree that the amount of disposable income that you have after taxes, bills and other expenses is your true net worth. That's because the more you earn, the more susceptible you are to lifestyle inflation. The more we have, the more we want, and the more we want, the more we spend. The cycle is wicked, and it can be everlasting. It breaks my heart to see people struggling financially because there is severe inequality in the American Dream. We live in a society in which the poor stay poor and the rich stay rich. Unfortunately, to some the dream is dead. The American Dream is the ability to climb the economic ladder and achieve more. Unfortunately, the speculative reality behind most people's perceptions is that to get rich you have to be famous, have a job that pays a hell of a lot of money, or win the lottery. Even those with a good education and a good job are feeling financially insecure. This goes against conventional wisdom, especially when we equate those who we perceive as being more educated with being financially smarter. Many people are waiting for the systems around them to change. To me this is a waste of time. In my opinion, it is easier to change myself. It's time for you to take control of your economic future. When money and power are at stake if you want to change your life, you will need to change your rules. In many ways, your current financial situation is not entirely your fault because most people are never taught how money works. Even though many people go to college and earn tens of thousands of dollars a year, we are ignorant because we haven't been taught the basics of credit management, investments, what to do with our checks once we receive them, how to plan our financial life and especially how to plan for retirement. Most people were never taught by family or by the educational system how to manage their financial resources, so they have become financial slaves. Think about it. Where did you receive your personal financial training? Haven't you really been trained by TV, advertising and the media on how you should live, what you should buy and what kind of American Dream you should be chasing? The ironic thing is that many people actually spend thousands of dollars and incur debt trying to get rich. What these people don't know is that they are most likely already rich. They just don't see their wealth. The question is are you keeping it or giving it away? Let me explain: Many people in America will earn hundreds of thousands of dollars over the course of their working lifetime. Unfortunately, they'll end up giving it to creditors because they don't recognize it for the wealth that it is. Becoming successful financially or otherwise isn't easy, but it's also not so difficult that you can't get there. While it will take some effort to realize your dream, all it takes are a few small, deliberate moves for you to reach your financial goal.

Life isn't fair and as long as we breathe the air of a capitalistic society, you will never get a seat at the table to participate in the game of

40

money unless you take it. If you really want to be a *RICH MOTHERF$CKER*, you should be rioting in the street. I don't mean looting and tearing shit up. What this means is that you should be so pissed off that you aren't where you want to be financially that you will do something about it. Every time I thought about not being self-reliant, my stomach hurt. I felt like I was going to throw up. Many of you feel this way right now. I personally don't foresee the elite knocking on your door inviting you to join their club. That means you and I must change instead. To do this you must exploit your own financial management for personal gain.

On Jay-Z's 4:44 album he has a song called The Story of OJ. The song has a lyric that says "You want to know what's more important than throwing money away in a strip club...credit! It's a great song with a lot of really important messages and although in the right hands and with the right mindset credit can be leveraged to create wealth, the underlying message that I want to convey to you through this quote is that the economy is designed to manipulate you into working yourself to exhaustion for a lifetime to accumulate wealth for the companies you do business with...not you. Think about that for a minute...There is a concerted effort being waged against you to take the wealth that you will produce over a lifetime away from you and the most common way people give up their wealth is by using credit. Using debt to finance your lifestyle is a prescription for poverty. If you eliminate debt, you'll have the cashflow to rapidly build wealth. That sounds so good, I want to say it again...If you eliminate debt, you'll have the cashflow to rapidly build wealth.

So, ask yourself, whose definition of wealth are you pursuing? If you stop giving your wealth away, it can accumulate to give you true freedom and even wealth. In my previous book *BAD A$$ CEO*, I taught you how to free yourself from financial slavery by using the debt-snowball method, debt stacking method or the Avalanche method. They are all similar in nature and the goal of the end result is the same...financial freedom through debt elimination. Regardless of which variation that you choose, it is the perfect way to shift your focus from how much you make or are trying to make to how much you can keep. Unfortunately, many people don't recognize this as a limitless opportunity. It takes someone with a vision of the possibilities to attain new levels in the game of money. Someone with the courage to live his or her dreams... A *RICH MOTHERF$CKER* if you will. Think of the following steps as kind of a blueprint for how to move in this direction.

STEP ONE: WHY THE FUCK DO YOU WANT TO BE FINANCIALLY FREE

Success is the best revenge and I am the type of guy who holds a grudge. Especially against all of the haters who tried to tell me that I couldn't do what I dreamed of doing. I know it sounds petty, but this revenge is what drives me...It's my "Why!" Why did I want to be financially free? So that I could say "Fuck You" to all the people who doubted me, who made faces and grunting sounds when I confidently told them what I was going to accomplish. And if I worked for them and they were in a supervisory position over me, they told me "No you can't do that" because they thought that their title and position gave them authority over my dreams. Judge me if you must, but it was my reality. I'm Ray Motherf$cking Bolden and it's what keeps my game on point. What's your why? To take the first step you need a strong, compelling reason.

STEP TWO: SHARPEN YOUR DON'T GIVE A FUCK SKILLS

There's no doubt in my mind that some people like having only one right answer. It makes life easier... at least on the surface. This means that there are millions of intelligent people walking around who have all the right answers, but who don't know how to think. As a result, they are financially trapped. Society has robbed them of their ability to think. In a world full of people who are too conventional in their thinking you must adopt an attitude that is opposite to how people think and operate. You have to go in the opposite direction and sometimes move before you think you are ready. I know you are skeptical about that statement, but the skills you have are more than adequate. You have to say to yourself "That may be standard operating procedure for them, but I'm a *RICH MOTHERF$CKER,* I don't have time for that shit." And since you want to be a *RICH MOTHERF$CKER* and I know you do, you don't have time for it either. There is a big difference between walking around saying you want a million dollars and having crystal clear intentions, a fierce desire and hell-bent action toward this specific goal. What is needed is a new skill set...a different mentality. A totally different concept of what to do. You have to get to the point were enough is enough and you're not going to take it anymore. You have to envision yourself with this money and the specific things and/or experiences it's going to provide because being able to see beyond what's right in front of you will bring you great power. It's a function of character and fearlessness and it is simply a choice you have to make. Nothing great ever happens until someone gets really pissed off and doesn't give a fuck anymore.

STEP THREE: BE THE
MOTHERF$CKER IN RICH MOTHERF$CKER

Society prefers to keep you in a dependent position. It is in their interest that you do not become self-reliant, so they will hoard information. You must secretly work against this and seize this information for yourself. Once I did this, the whole world seemed to open up for me. For the first time in my life, I had stepped into a new world, the world of my dreams. Even though I wasn't creating the system, I found ways to make it my own. Nothing else existed. Nobody could tell me I wasn't right where I was supposed to be. You say you want wealth, but on the inside, you believe you can't have it. You don't believe that you can achieve it. With this type of thinking you are beaten before you even start. Here's the truth as I know it. I tried it their way, but it just didn't work for me. So, I developed my own way. In a conscious move to protect myself I put myself above the crowd in order to lead. I became the Alpha dog. You should give it a try as a professional courtesy. We can't allow our perception of circumstances to form our reality. Having clarity about where you are headed and what is happening in the world around you translates into confidence and power. Once you taste this power, you will find more satisfaction... propelling you to reach for more. From that moment on, you'll know what you want, and you'll know how to make it happen. All that matters is what's true for you and if you can stay connected to that without straying, you will be the MOTHERF$CKER in *RICH MOTHERF$CKER*.

THE POWER IS YOURS NOT THEIRS

I know that this approach and these general rules of thumb and formulas don't always speak to your particular situation. If you're like most people, you've hit a few bumps along the road, emergencies pop up, your kids cost more than you ever dreamed, and your bank account never seems to be quite as large as you hope... but you can't solve the puzzle by staying inside your customary frame of reference. Unless we change our thinking, it won't matter how much money we make. We have to change our entire mind-set. If we can change how we think, we will change our lives. Being a *RICH MOTHERF$CKER* means you are able to step back from your assumptions and emotions about money and observe them objectively. Actually doing the simple steps outlined here will transform your relationship with money. You will go from *RICH MOTHERF$CKER* thinking to *RICH MOTHERF$CKER* living and *RICH MOTHERF$CKER* thinking will naturally lead to financial intelligence, financial integrity and financial independence. There is a quote that says, "A people who do not see themselves as a nation may not act in its own best interest." Therefore, the only strategy that I can provide to address the issue is to educate you on your own identity, purpose and direction and attempt to get you to look at your values from a freedom and self-sufficiency point of view. I pray that my solutions will be implemented. Here's how it works: The difference between those who find the best of times and those who find the worst of times is simply the mentality of being a *RICH MOTHERF$CKER*. It's so easy once you figure out that it's not hard. You can be a *RICH MOTHERF$CKER* if you believe in yourself and are willing to put action behind the knowledge you gain. This would make you instantly wealthy in a way that you have never dared contemplate. You can take control of your financial future if you are willing to learn, take action, make mistakes, learn from those mistakes and shift your focus from how much you can make to how much you can keep.

"RICH MOTHERF$CKER" – EXERCISE APPENDIX - B

The median household income in America is about $59,000. Multiply that by an average 40 year working life and you'll see that the average household will make $2,360,000 in a lifetime. Imagine for a minute what it would be like to keep most of that because you don't have to worry about paying bills. What would that feel like? Who would you be?

Ask yourself the following questions to discover the limitless possibilities. These questions will help you focus on what you truly value and what makes your life worth living. The point is to clear out all the distractions and rationalizations and all the bullshit we tell ourselves. Allow yourself to be pissed off and don't give a fuck anymore, but in a positive way. Don't allow your mind to justify your current situation and over time amazing changes will occur...not only in your relationship with money, but in your relationship with life itself.

- The amount of my current income is? (Keep in mind that there are people who aren't any smarter than you making billions) How do you feel about making this amount?

- Multiply your annual salary by the number of years you plan to work until you retire. Describe in detail how it would feel to keep most of it because you don't have to pay bills. What would it feel like? Who would you be?

- How does it feel to live like you make less income than you actually do because you're in debt?

- The total amount I pay out in bills / owe in debts is? How pissed off are you about having to pay this much? How stupid you do feel about getting into debt?

- Write a "I'm pissed off and I don't give a fuck anymore" statement. Example: I'm pissed off and I don't give a fuck anymore… I will not continue to live paycheck to paycheck, losing sleep wondering how I'm going to make ends meet etc. (The more detailed the statement the better)

PART THREE

Look beyond what's right in front of you

RICH MOTHERF$CKER!

"There are two types of Kings in this world: The ones who are given their crowns and the ones who take them."

~ Chrysler 300 Ad

Chapter Three

CREATE YOUR
OWN RELIGION

(Be smarter, wiser and do it your way)

With technology replacing people in the workforce, global competition, unemployment and less job security, people dream of being their own boss, starting their own business and enjoying a life of financial freedom. So, at this very moment because you want to be a *RICH MOTHERF$CKER*, you are asking yourself, "What can I do?" The answer is there are many things that you can do. The world is full of problems so a better question might be "What problem can I solve?" What problem or problems do you think God gave you unique gifts to solve? To me, these aren't just rhetorical questions. I've had to answer them. When you look at the world from the point of view of problems to solve, you will see that there is a lot to do and a lot that you can do. The more important question is: "Are you willing to work on solving the problem?"

I encourage you to read my books *BAD BOYS FINI$H RICH* and *REBELLIOU$ WEALTH* if you want to see entrepreneurship, self-reliance and economic empowerment from a different point of view. I recommend these books because when I started I didn't have any qualifications to educate others. I was only doing what I saw needed to be done...solving a problem if you will; which was to provide a different kind of education and be a different kind of role model for anyone and everyone who wants to learn self-reliance and entrepreneurship. Some people are gifted at specific things, but I had to develop the thing I'm most talented at. Through all my ups and downs, it was the creation of my own personal brand and discovering my authenticity that helped me live my version of the American Dream. Not just settling for the bullshit information and images of success that were being presented to me...not just checking off boxes of what others perception of success looks like and not just accepting society's label of who I was supposed to be, definitely played into my motivation. You only have so many minutes in every day... so many ticks on the clock and every action you perform means by definition, you're not performing some other action. You have to make choices, and it was time I made mine. I don't want to leave this planet until I achieve everything that I was put here to do so with unquenchable faith and unflinching will, I set myself to the task. My passion for self-reliance often out ran my capacities but I persevered and spent more than ten years giving my brand sound footing. My purpose was revealed in my nakedly simple slogan: *"BAD BOYS FINI$H RICH!"* It is intentionally self-referential. Incorporating the spirit of who I am prominently into the design of my books. It was the brand I was born into from supervisors who labeled me a "Bad Boy" and "not a team player." When your dream is bigger than others dreams there are always going to be people who consider themselves smarter than you about what it takes to be successful. It unlocked the code from average to great and it was my personal revolt against others controlling my life. By solving a problem, I walked into my former employer's offices as an employee, but I walked out as something more.

As a *RICH MOTHERF$CKER*, you trumpet your individuality and take great pride in your accomplishments. If others cannot accept that or judge you as arrogant, that is their problem, not yours. As I was on this journey, change was occurring and I found myself aligned with forces that were driving me along new paths. I was awed by the power that I held in my hands. According to Novelist Richard Bach, "You are never given a wish without also being given the power to make it true." So, it didn't make sense to have a small view of what's possible. The problems I solved allow me to be an author, business owner and serial-entrepreneur. The problem and the solution are usually obvious and simple. It's not that you don't know what to do. Of course, you do. You are just terrified that you might end up worse off than you are now. You must always be prepared to bet on yourself and on your future, by heading in a direction that others seem to fear. The higher your self-belief, the more power you have to transform reality.

BE THE SUCCESS STORY THAT'S TAKING PLACE RIGHT IN FRONT OF YOU

There is a perception that it's more lucrative, less demanding and more financially rewarding to work for someone else than to own your own business. This is a slave mentality of supporting and working for others versus ourselves. Any time you focus only on consuming, you have nothing to be proud of, other than what you consume. If you don't produce and simply wait for someone to hire you, and give you a vision, you may not get there. We must be active participants in the multi-trillion dollar global economy. Now is the time to educate yourself...to teach yourself to be employers rather than employees and producers rather than consumers. The question becomes, "How do I rise to such a prominent position?" The heaviness of success-chasing can be replaced with a serendipitous lightness when you recognize that the only rules and limits are those we set for ourselves. You must create the proper leverage to be unshackled. Being a *RICH MOTHERF$CKER* gives you a sense of purpose that guides you but doesn't chain you to one way of doing things. And when your *RICH MOTHERF$CKER* mindset is deeply engaged, it will push you past any limits. Once you realize that you can solve problems and sell the solution you are liberated in a way that few people ever know. It's the simplest route to profitability.

CAPITALISM AT IT'S FINEST

Nothing I teach is difficult, It's just different. The idea of being a *RICH MOTHERF$CKER* is simple and straight forward. It's modeled to stand out from the crowd, structured to encourage an entrepreneurial spirit, study business principles and develop a product or service that will be demanded in the international market. So, ask yourself: "What are my strengths, weaknesses and talents, and what problems can I solve to create products and services that I can I bring to the world's table for consumption?" It is important for you... like corporations, to assess yourself and leverage your strengths and weaknesses economically, because we are *RICH MOTHERF$CKER*s, and *RICH MOTHERF$CKER*s take a problem, find the solution, build a business that turns solutions into products...and these products become money. Our wealth is not in the money; our wealth is in the ownership of solutions.

"RICH MOTHERF$CKER" – EXERCISE APPENDIX-C

The ability to solve problems can make you a *RICH MOTHERF$CKER*. If you can solve your customer's problems, you could convince them to buy almost anything. By answering the following questions, brainstorming and some real-life observation, you can develop products by solving problems and selling the solution.

- This product is for: (Who will buy this product. Be specific.)

- It will help them solve this problem: (Describe the problem your customers are looking to solve.)

- I expect my product to: (Explain how your solution will solve their problem in a meaningful and valuable way.)

- I am doing this because: (What's your vision behind it?)

- This is how I will do this: (What is your strategy?)

PART FOUR

Own your identity and flip it on them

RICH MOTHERF$CKER!

"Men suffer more from imagining too little than too much."

~*P.T. Barnum*

Chapter Four

WRITTEN, DIRECTED AND
STARRED IN BY RAY BOLDEN

(Teach yourself to live well)

Many people are just waiting to be discovered.. waiting for that one big break. But a man's position in life is limited only by his imagination. People say that what we are seeking is a meaning for life. I don't think this is what we're really looking for. I think what we're searching for is the experience of being alive. I believe that life exists to be enjoyed and that the most important thing is to feel good about yourself. My calling is to tell people the truth about self-reliance and entrepreneurship and give them the hope and tools to set themselves free financially. Being a genius and all, and I don't say that lightly, I was captivated by the idea that the answers I desired about my purpose might in fact be inside me. I was searching for stability, a sense of clarity and inner peace. As I searched, I wrote, and my concept jumped off the page and into my soul...propelling me to reach for more and revolutionizing my thinking forever. As a result, my books are extreme and so am I, so this is my personal playbook for the game known as *RICH MOTHERF$CKER*. It's obvious that I wanted to tell my story, but in my words. This was that story. I never at any point entertained the possibility of not using this title because it is not my job to provide you with comfort. I wasn't trying to create controversy for the sake of controversy. Outrage, self-righteousness and titillation all work equally well. I understood that some people would find it provocative because the term can be an insult, describing despicable grandiosity and a disregard for others, but it can also be the ultimate compliment, indicating a mastery of your art. In these words, many are confronted by everything they have ever aspired to be and the reality of what they may never become. The negativity means I am touching a nerve that needs to be touched in order for you to change your life and I use the anger and criticism as encouragement. You have read about my concept...a proven plan to win. The plan is very simple yet inspiring. I am convinced that my plan will work for everyone because *RICH MOTHERF$CKER* is the culmination of power and class...the individual versus authority and being a *RICH MOTHERF$CKER* is the by-product of diligently following the steps of the principles outlined in this book. I strongly urge you to take notes while reading this book because this is not a one-time read. You need to read this book over and over again until you fully understand it. I'm very excited because I know this book will inspire readers to take immediate action through a simple step-by-step process that could only lead to life-changing results. I have told you what I do, but that doesn't mean I recommend that you do what I do, because what I do is rather sophisticated. It has taken me years to learn how to do it. In fact, I'm still learning. I'm telling you about it so that you can see the other side. If you can see what most people never see, you will better understand how the real game is played. This is an overly simplified explanation of a very complex process, but if you follow the diagram, your mind will see the invisible world of *RICH MOTHERF$CKERs* that very few people ever see. If you doubt that it can happen then you are right. If you can see it happening, then you will do everything you need to do in order to make it happen. So, look inside and pay attention to your instincts.

IF YOU HAVE NEVER BEEN EDUCATED BY A RICH MOTHERF$CKER, YOU'VE NEVER BEEN EDUCATED AT ALL

Most people want to be spoon fed from television and the media instead of reading this book to learn and gain the understanding needed for the next opportunity. What are you preparing for in your life? Are you prepared? How much time did you spend last week getting ready for the next opportunity that will come along in your life? How many books have you read this year? When was the last time you bought a book, read it, took notes and studied it? To become a *RICH MOTHERF$CKER* you have to be fully committed. If you aren't going to be fully committed to the whole process, don't even start.

Many of you picked up this book with false expectations that the book will do the work for you, but the road is yours to travel alone. The problem is and has always been we don't see ourselves as *RICH MOTHERF$CKERs*. Do we feel it isn't significant enough? How do we enforce the execution of this idea? I realize that I'm making it sound like we're all crazy, but that's because we kind of are. Until we wake up, which is what this book will hopefully help you do, life can be extremely illogical and unreasonable. In each of my books, you will find one or two pieces of the puzzle and the book you are reading now will help to put all of those puzzle pieces together. In case I'm not painting the picture correctly, to win the game, you got to be in it and to be counted, you got to participate. So why do we spend more time talking about the problem than working on the solution? Is it ignorance? Fear? Why have we not moved from theory to practice? Always remember, there is a big difference between knowing how to take confident action and waiting to be told what to do.

THE NEXT RICH MOTHERF$CKER

I'm not naïve enough to think that we are all in agreement on these principles. Ninety-six percent of Americans fail to achieve true financial independence, so I accept the reality that the majority of my readers are not going to become *RICH MOTHERF$CKERs*. To those who choose to disparage the 'simple' truths within, I would simply ask how far along on your own paths are you that you are still looking for complicated answers? The 'secret' is hidden in plain sight. You've probably heard that a million times. The trick, however, is in putting this book down after you've read it and taking action...something this book inspires you to do. That's the true value of it.

I was someone who saw the world in widescreen Cinemascope Technicolor. The rest of the world was too slow. I had no vehicle for articulating my grievances, no public defender, so I went on a quest to find out how to be self-reliant and how money really works so I could take control of it and have confidence handling it. I was aware that a metamorphosis was taking place inside of me. More importantly, I knew my self-reliance was growing. The interesting thing is that I feel that if I had more of the discipline of formal education, I would have achieved less because I would have been restrained by history and precedent. I did in-depth, detailed research and found that I was packing an extremely powerful weapon. My vision represented tremendous long-term opportunity. For the first time I saw a world that was bigger than the one I had been born into and I wanted more. Up until this point I had viewed wealth as unattainable. That's what I thought, until I met my mentor in the mirror. Our meeting created an enormous incubator for success, intellectual thought and creativity. Lack of success is self-imposed, and freedom is something you can only give yourself, so the reason I write books is to teach and give others the same opportunity that my mentor-in-the mirror gave me. By searching deep within, I discovered that I was in the presence of someone I wanted to emulate. This wasn't just a legend in front of me...this was a God. I took ownership of the trademark that was given to me by previous supervisors and flipped it on them. Because with the right mindset *BAD BOYS FINI$H RICH.* I solved problems for myself and others and invented money that already existed, allowing me to create *REBELLIOU$ WEALTH.* Most of all, I sharpened my don't give a fuck skills, went left when everybody else went right, and taught myself to live well, by playing the game in my own way, because I was a *BAD A$$ CEO.* And That ladies and gentlemen is how I became... a *RICH MOTHERF$CKER!* I challenge you to look inside yourself and discover, once and for all, who you can become. I truly believe that once you discover the full value of the *RICH MOTHERF$CKER* mindset. you will become not only who you were meant to become... you will become more than you ever dreamed!

FOLLOW RAY ON SOCIAL MEDIA

PERSPECTIVES ON FINANCIAL LITERACY AND ENTREPRENEURIAL EDUCATION THAT OFTEN CONTRADICT CONVENTIONAL WISDOM

Follow Ray on Facebook:

www.facebook.com/boldambitionworldwide

Follow Ray on Instagram:

www.instagram.com/badboysfinishrich

Follow Ray on Twitter:

www.twitter.com/IamMrBolden

Follow Ray on Amazon:
www.amazon.com/Ray-Bolden/e/B00VXC3YN4/ref=ntt_dp_epwbk_0
Please Note: After enjoying Ray's work, please provide a customer review and give feedback on Amazon.com.

Visit BADBOYSFINISHRICH.COM/#social

From RAY BOLDEN, Author of the Best Seller "BAD BOYS FINISH RICH"

A BOOK FOR A VIDEO

BE A PART OF THE THOUSANDS OF LIVES CHANGED WITH THE HELP OF THE BAD BOYS FINI$H RICH PRINCIPLES!

Here's How It Works:

1. Once you receive your book, create a video of you holding up the book and enthusiastically saying the following:

I'm (First & Last Name) from (City & State or City and Country)! "Bad Boys or Bad Girls" Finish Rich! (Based on your gender)
I Got My Copy, Get Yours!

2. Post the video on Youtube.com.

3. Email the link of your video to admin@badboysfinishrich.com.
Once we receive your video link and verify it for clarity and authenticity, we will add it to our growing list of videos.

Please Note: Please follow the script provided above. We reserve the right to reject and refuse any videos deemed substandard or inappropriate.

Visit **BADBOYSFINISHRICH.COM** for Examples!

BAD BOYS FINISH RICH

BOLD AMBITION

WORLDWIDE